FAVOURITE
NORTHUM ... PES

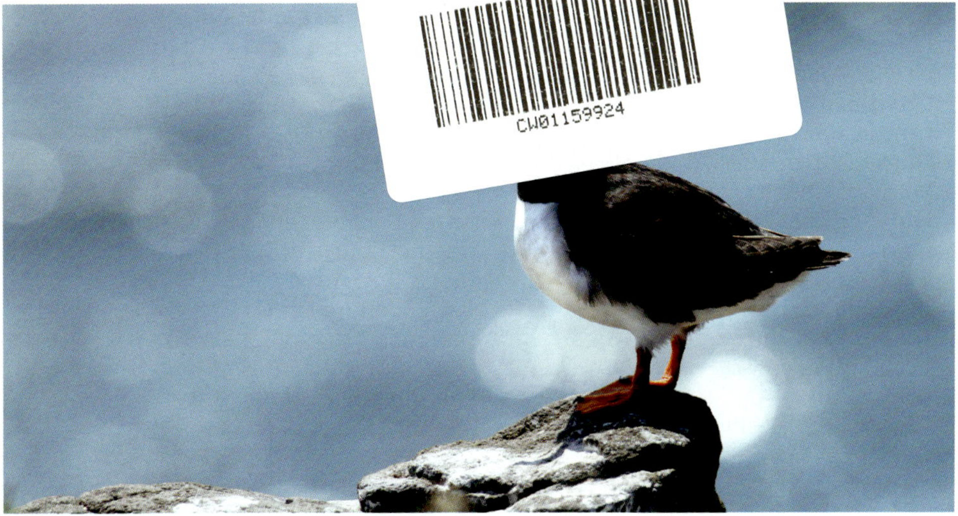

Dorrigo

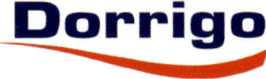

Index

Alnwick Stew 45
Bacon Floddies 38
Carlings 24
Celery Cheese 43
Cockle Soup 19
Courting Cake 7
Cousin Jim 22
Curd Cheesecakes 23
Durham Cutlets 35
Durham Lunch Cake 8
Durham Pikelets 14
Durham Popovers 21
Felton Spice Loaf 34
Kipper Paste 6
Leek Pudding 37
Lemon Cake 42
Newcastle Pease Pudding 26

Newcastle Pudding 10
North Country Tart 40
Northumbrian Girdle Cakes 5
Northumberland Twists 11
Oven Bottom Cake 39
Overnight Spice Cake 30
Pan Haggerty 3
Panjotheram 32
Pot Pie 27
Potted Salmon 16
Singin' Hinnies 13
South Tyne Yeast Cake 18
Stanhope Firelighters 15
Stanhope Fruit and Nut Cake 31
Tasty Batter Pudding 47
Threshing Day Barley Bread 29
Whitley Goose 46

Printed & published by Dorrigo, Manchester, England © Copyright
All rights reserved. No part of this publication may be reproduced, stored in a retrieval system or transmitted, in any form or by means, electronic, mechanical, photocopying or otherwise. Recipes J Salmon Ltd, Images Adobe Stock

Pan Haggerty

A popular Northumberland supper dish, said to have taken its name from the French 'hachis', meaning to chop or slice. Traditionally Pan Haggerty is always served direct from the pan in which it is cooked.

2 tablespoons oil or 1 oz dripping   1 lb potatoes, peeled and thinly sliced
2 medium onions, peeled and thinly sliced   4 oz grated cheese; preferably Lancashire
Salt and black pepper

Heat the oil or dripping in a large frying pan. Place the sliced potatoes in a layer over the base of the pan and cover with the sliced onions. Season and sprinkle over the grated cheese. Cover the frying pan with a lid and fry gently for 30 minutes or until cooked through. Remove the lid and either turn the mixture in the pan to brown the top or place under a hot grill to brown the cheese. Serve in wedges direct from the pan. Serves 4 to 6.

A very similar supper dish, which additionally contains chopped bacon, is popular in County Durham. Known as Panackelty, it too is served direct from the pan in which it is cooked.

Northumbrian Girdle Cakes

These cakes, containing currants, are also known as Gosforth Gridies.

1 lb self-raising flour
1 teaspoon salt
8 oz butter
4 oz sugar
4 oz currants
2 eggs, beaten
5 fl oz milk

Sift the flour and salt together in a bowl, then rub in the butter until the mixture resembles fine breadcrumbs. Add the sugar and currants, then make a well in the mixture and add the eggs and milk. Stir the mixture with a round-bladed knife until well-combined. Turn out on to a lightly floured surface and knead lightly, then roll out to approximately ½-inch thick. Cut into small rounds and bake on a hot, well-greased griddle or frying pan for 4 to 5 minutes on each side, until golden brown. Serve hot, with butter.

Lindisfarne Castle

Kipper Paste

From the 19th century, Northumberland had a flourishing kipper industry, for which the picturesque harbour of Craster was especially renowned.

2 medium kippers
5 oz unsalted butter
1 dessertspoon lemon juice

Pinch cayenne pepper
Salt and black pepper
Melted butter

Stand the kippers in a jug of boiling water for 10 to 12 minutes. Then drain well, remove the skin and all the bones and flake the flesh. Cut the butter into cubes and place in a saucepan over a low heat until half-melted, then remove from the heat and whisk until completely melted. Add the flaked kipper and combine very well with a fork until the mixture is smooth – alternatively use a liquidiser. Stir in the lemon juice and season with cayenne pepper and a little salt and black pepper. Place in small pots and press down well. Spoon the melted butter over the mixture to seal and leave to set. Serve well chilled as a starter, with buttered crusty bread or toast, or use as a sandwich filling.

Courting Cake

Courting cakes were traditionally made by newly-engaged girls to impress their betrothed. Versions appear all over Britain, but they are particularly popular in Northern counties.

8 oz butter, softened
8 oz caster sugar
4 eggs, beaten
12 oz self-raising flour
3 tablespoons milk
10 fl oz double cream
8 oz strawberries, washed, hulled and sliced
A little sifted icing sugar

Set oven to 375°F or Mark 5. Grease and base-line three 7-inch sandwich tins. Cream the butter and sugar together in a bowl until light and fluffy. Add the eggs, a little at a time with a little flour, beating well between each addition. Fold in the remaining flour and stir in the milk to give a soft, dropping consistency. Divide the mixture evenly between the tins and bake for 25 to 30 minutes until well-risen and springy to the touch – it is advisable to exchange the position of the top and bottom tins during cooking. Turn out the cakes on to a wire rack to cool. Whip the cream until it stands in soft peaks. Sandwich the cakes together with the cream and the sliced strawberries and dredge the top with a little icing sugar.

Although strawberries are most usually used, raspberries, blackberries etc. can be substituted, if desired.

Durham Lunch Cake

Lunch cakes were developed in the 18th century as something to enjoy as a snack to be eaten before an early evening dinner. This is a substantial fruit cake.

**1 lb plain flour   ¼ teaspoon of salt   ¾ oz baking powder
3 oz lard   3 oz margarine or butter   6 oz caster sugar
½ lb currants   ¼ lb sultanas   ¼ lb raisins
Grated rind of a lemon   2 teaspoons lemon juice
2 teaspoons ground nutmeg   2 teaspoons ground cinnamon
2 teaspoons mixed spice   ½ level teaspoon ground cloves
2 eggs, beaten   6 fl oz milk**

Set oven to 350°F or Mark 4. Grease and base-line a 9 or 10-inch cake tin. Sift the flour, salt and baking powder together into a bowl, then rub in the fat until the mixture resembles fine breadcrumbs. Stir in the sugar, fruit, lemon rind and juice and spices, then add the eggs, a little at a time and mix to a dropping consistency with the milk. Turn the mixture into the cake tin and smooth over the top. Bake for 2 hours, covering the top with a piece of kitchen foil if it appears to be browning too quickly. Cool in the tin for 10 minutes, then turn out on to a wire rack.

Alnwick Castle

Newcastle Pudding

A steamed form of bread-and-butter pudding served with lemon sauce.

**¾ pint milk   Grated rind of a lemon   3 eggs, beaten   2 oz sugar
6 slices white bread, thickly buttered with crusts removed**

Warm the milk in a pan and stir in the lemon rind. Cover and leave to infuse for 1 hour. Beat the eggs and sugar well together, then pour into the milk and whisk well together. Line a well-buttered 1½ to 2-pint pudding basin with the slices of bread, buttered side inwards. Strain the milk mixture and leave to soak for 1 hour. Cover with buttered greaseproof paper and kitchen foil and tie down. Place the pudding basin in a saucepan of boiling water and steam for 40 to 45 minutes, topping up the water as necessary. Turn out the pudding on to a warm serving dish and serve with lemon sauce. Serves 4.

FOR THE LEMON SAUCE

2 oz caster sugar   1 pint water   Rind and juice of a lemon   2 eggs, beaten   3 oz butter

Boil the sugar, water and lemon rind and juice together in a saucepan until slightly reduced and thickened. Pour into a double saucepan or a bowl in a pan filled with boiling water and stir in the beaten eggs and butter. Bring back to the boil and whisk continuously until the sauce thickens. Strain into a warm jug or sauce-boat and serve hot. This is a slightly tart sauce.

Northumberland Twists

A yeast-cake dough, cut into strips and brushed with sherry prior to twisting and baking.

1 lb strong white flour
2 oz caster sugar
4 oz butter, melted
¼ pint warm water
¼ oz dried yeast
3 tablespoons sherry
A little caster sugar

Stir the flour and sugar together in a warm bowl, then add the melted butter and combine well. Mix 2 tablespoons of the warm water with the yeast and let it stand for a few minutes until frothy. Add to the flour mixture with the remainder of the water and combine well. Turn out on to a lightly floured surface and knead until smooth and elastic. Form into a ball, place in a bowl and cover with a clean tea-towel. Leave in a warm place for 1½ to 2 hours until doubled in bulk. Set oven to 375°F or Mark 5. Turn out the dough on to a lightly floured surface and knead well, then roll out and cut into strips approximately 4 inches long and ½ inch wide. Twist each strip slightly and divide between 2 well-greased baking sheets. Brush the twists with sherry and sprinkle with caster sugar, then bake for 20 to 25 minutes until golden. Eat freshly baked and slightly warm.

Singin' Hinnies

A fried scone that gained its name because it 'sings' and sizzles while cooking.
'Hinny' is a Northern term of endearment used especially to children.

8 oz plain flour
Pinch of salt
1 teaspoon baking powder
2 oz butter
2 oz lard
1 oz sugar
3 oz currants or sultanas
2-3 tablespoons milk

Sift the flour, salt and baking powder together into a bowl, then rub in the butter and lard until the mixture resembles fine breadcrumbs. Stir in the sugar and fruit and mix to a stiff dough with the milk. Roll into a ball, then turn out on to a lightly floured surface and flatten into a round cake about ½-inch thick. Lightly grease and heat a frying pan or griddle and place on it the hinny. Prick the top lightly with a fork and cook for 15 to 20 minutes, turning once, until golden brown on both sides. Serve hot, cut into wedges and spread with plenty of butter.

Warkworth Castle

Durham Pikelets

Pikelet is a regional name for a crumpet.

**8 oz plain flour   1 teaspoon bicarbonate of soda
1 teaspoon cream of tartar   ½ teaspoon salt   1½ oz lard
8 to 10 fl oz buttermilk or semi-skimmed milk**

Sift the flour, bicarbonate of soda, cream of tartar and salt together into a bowl, then rub in the lard until the mixture resembles fine breadcrumbs. Make a well in the centre and add the buttermilk or milk, beating lightly to give a dropping consistency. Drop the mixture, in spoonfuls, on to a hot, well-greased griddle or frying pan and cook the pikelets for about 4 minutes on each side until golden brown. Keep warm, wrapped in a clean, warm tea-towel and serve hot, spread with butter.

Stanhope Firelighters

A form of flapjack traditional to County Durham.

8 oz rolled oats **4 oz brown sugar**
8 oz margarine, melted **4 oz white sugar**

Set oven to 350°F or Mark 4. In a bowl, blend the oats and margarine well together. Mix the sugars together and stir into the mixture, combining well. Press the mixture into a well-greased Swiss roll tin and bake for 25 to 30 minutes. Mark into squares in the tin while still hot and remove when cool.

Potted Salmon

Potted salmon was very popular in the 18th century. There are a number of recipe variations and this one comes from Newcastle.

4 salmon steaks – approx. 6 oz each in weight
White pepper   2 oz butter
½ oz spice made up of ground mace and cloves, well mixed together
Melted butter

Set oven to 350°F or Mark 4. Wipe the salmon steaks and season with the spices and a little pepper. Place in a well-buttered ovenproof dish and dot with butter. Cover with a lid or a piece of kitchen foil and bake for 30 to 40 minutes, occasionally basting the steaks with the liquid. Lift out the salmon steaks and drain well. Allow to cool a little, then remove all skin and bones and flake the flesh finely. Place in 4 to 6 ramekin dishes and press down well. Spoon the melted butter over the fish to seal, and leave to set. Serve well chilled, as a starter, with buttered crusty bread or toast.

Hexham Abbey

South Tyne Yeast Cake

Traditional to County Durham, this cake should be kept for at least a week before eating.

**4 oz butter   4 oz sugar   1 egg, beaten   4 oz currants   4 oz sultanas
2 oz chopped mixed peel   ¼ oz dried yeast, dissolved in 2½ fl oz soured milk
¼ teaspoon bicarbonate of soda, dissolved in 2½ fl oz cold milk
8 oz plain flour**

FOR THE GLAZE

1 tablespoon warm milk in which 1 teaspoon of sugar has been dissolved

Cream the butter and sugar together in a bowl until light and fluffy, then beat in the egg and stir in the fruit and peel. Add the flour, alternately with the yeast and bicarbonate of soda mixtures and combine well. Turn out on to a lightly floured surface and knead to a smooth, soft dough. Place in a well-greased 1 lb loaf tin, cover with a clean tea-towel and leave in a warm place for about 30 minutes or until doubled in bulk. Set oven to 350°F or Mark 4. Bake for 2 hours, covering the top with kitchen foil if it appears to be browning too quickly. Turn out of the tin, brush the top with the glaze and leave to cool on a wire rack.

Cockle Soup

Originally the cockles for this Northumberland soup were boiled in sea water.

**40-50 cockles   1 oz butter   1 oz plain flour   1 pint full cream milk
2 tablespoons finely chopped onion   2 tablespoons finely chopped celery
2 tablespoons chopped fresh parsley   Black pepper
A little chopped fresh parsley for garnish   Cream for serving**

Scrub the cockle shells very well under cold running water, discarding any that are already open. Place the cockles in a large saucepan and cover with cold, well-salted water. Bring slowly to the boil, shaking the saucepan from time to time. As soon as the cockles are open they are ready; do not over-cook, as this will toughen them. Allow the cockles to cool in the stock, then strain, reserving the stock, and remove the cockles from their shells using a sharp knife. Strain the cooled stock again and make up to 1½ pints with water if necessary. Melt the butter in a saucepan, stir in the flour and cook for 1 minute. Gradually add the cockle stock, stirring to prevent lumps forming. Bring to the boil, then stir in the milk. Add the onion and celery and cook, stirring, for 5-10 minutes or until the vegetables are soft. Add the parsley and black pepper, then stir in the cockles. Heat through thoroughly and pour into 4 to 6 soup bowls. Swirl a tablespoon of cream into each bowl and garnish with a little parsley. Serve with crusty bread.

Nineteen

Durham Popovers

A rich, egg batter pudding often served at breakfast-time with marmalade or preserves.

**½ lb plain flour   4 eggs, beaten
1 oz butter   Pinch of salt
A little milk**

Set oven to 425°F or Mark 7. Sift the flour into a bowl, then rub in the butter. Make a well in the centre and stir in the beaten eggs and the salt, then add sufficient milk to make a smooth, creamy batter. Spoon into 12 to 14 well-greased patty tins, filling them just half-full and bake for 30 minutes, until well risen and golden. Serve hot with jam or marmalade.

Blanchland

Cousin Jim

A liver and bacon dish traditional to County Durham.

1 lb liver	**½ pint beef stock**
½ lb bacon, de-rinded	**½ - ¾ lb potatoes, peeled**
4 onions, peeled and sliced	**and sliced**
Salt and black pepper	**A little melted butter**

Set oven to 350°F or Mark 4. Wipe and trim the liver, then cut into thin slices and dust with a little seasoned flour. In a frying pan, fry the bacon lightly in its own fat. Remove the bacon, add sufficient cooking oil and lightly fry the liver and onions. Arrange the liver, onions and bacon in an ovenproof dish, seasoning well. Pour on the stock and top with the sliced potatoes. Cover with a lid or a piece of kitchen foil and bake for about 1 hour. Remove the lid or foil during the final 20 minutes of cooking and brush the potatoes with melted butter to brown. Serve with carrots or a green vegetable. Serves 4 to 6.

Curd Cheesecakes

Individual tarts filled with a curd mixture containing ground almonds, currants, spices and sherry.

6 oz prepared shortcrust pastry

6 oz curd cheese	**1 tablespoon double cream**
3 oz butter, softened	**¼ teaspoon ground nutmeg**
2 oz caster sugar	**1 teaspoon ground cinnamon**
1 oz ground almonds	**2 eggs, beaten**
4 oz currants	**2½ fl oz sherry**

A little sifted icing sugar

Set oven to 350°F or Mark 4. Roll out the pastry on a lightly floured surface and use to line 12 to 14 patty tins. In a bowl, beat the curd cheese until smooth, then beat in the butter. Add the sugar, almonds, currants, cream and spices and combine very well together. Then stir in the beaten eggs and sherry. Spoon the mixture into the pastry cases, smooth the tops and bake for 15 to 20 minutes or until golden. Cool on a wire rack. Serve sprinkled with icing sugar.

Carlings

This Northumberland dish takes its name from the Old English word for 'mourning'. It was traditionally served on Passion – or Carling – Sunday, when church altars were draped in purple in mourning for the memory of Christ's Passion. Dishes containing peas were regularly eaten during Lent, when meat was forbidden.

8 oz dried green peas
2 oz fresh white breadcrumbs
1 medium onion, peeled and finely chopped
½ teaspoon mixed herbs
Salt and black pepper
1 tablespoon melted butter
1 oz butter for frying

Soak the peas overnight in cold water. The next morning, drain and rinse well. Place in a large saucepan and cover with 1½ pints cold water. Bring to the boil and boil for 1½ to 2 hours, stirring regularly and adding extra water if necessary, until the peas are tender. Leave to cool, then in a bowl mix the peas with the breadcrumbs, onion, herbs, seasoning and melted butter to form a stiff mixture. Shape into cakes and dust lightly with a little seasoned flour. Melt the 1 oz butter in a frying pan and fry the Carlings until golden brown, turning once. Serve immediately. Serves 4.

Although not traditional, Carlings can be served as an accompaniment to gammon, ham or grilled bacon.

Craster

Newcastle Pease Pudding

Pease pudding dates back to medieval days and traditionally has always been eaten with pork. In the 19th century 'Pease Pudding Hot…' was sold by street vendors – especially in and around Newcastle. It was, and still is, very much a North-eastern dish.

1 pint split peas   1 large egg, beaten
2 oz butter, softened   A little extra butter
Salt and black pepper

Soak the peas overnight in cold water. The next morning, rinse well and tie loosely in a pudding cloth. Place in a saucepan of boiling water and boil for 2 hours, topping up the water as necessary. Drain well, allow to cool a little, and then rub through a sieve. Put the sieved peas in a bowl, beat in the butter and seasoning, then stir in the egg, combining the mixture well together. Set oven to 350°F or Mark 4. Turn the mixture into a well-buttered ovenproof dish and smooth the top. Dot with a little butter and bake for 25 to 30 minutes, covering with a piece of kitchen foil to prevent it browning too quickly. Serve with roast pork, accompanied by roast potatoes and cabbage. Serves 4.

Pot Pie

This is a County Durham version of steak and kidney pudding.

1 lb stewing steak	½ lb prepared suet pastry
½ lb kidney, wiped and cored	½ pint beef stock
2 onions, peeled and chopped	Salt and black pepper
2 tablespoons chopped fresh parsley	

Cut the steak and kidney into 1-inch cubes and dust lightly with a little seasoned flour. Layer half the meat, half the onion and half the parsley in a 2½ to 3-pint pudding basin, seasoning each layer. Roll out the pastry on a lightly floured surface and cut off a strip about 2 inches wide and sufficiently long to fit round the inside of the basin. Use this to line the top part of the basin, sealing the ends well together. Layer the remaining meat, onion and parsley, seasoning the layers and pour in the stock. Roll out the remainder of the pastry and cut out a lid to fit. Use this to cover the basin, sealing the edges well together, then tie down with a piece of buttered greaseproof paper, topped with a piece of kitchen foil. Steam for 3½ to 4 hours in a saucepan of boiling water, topping up the water as necessary. Serve with boiled potatoes and vegetables. Serves 4 to 6.

Threshing Day Barley Bread

A scone-like bread baked on a griddle and made at threshing time in Northumberland.

1 lb barley flour	2 teaspoons cream of tartar
4 oz plain flour	1 pint buttermilk or milk
1 teaspoon salt	A little beaten egg

1 teaspoon bicarbonate of soda

Set oven at 475°F or Mark 9. In a bowl, mix together the flours, salt, bicarbonate of soda and cream of tartar. Then stir in the buttermilk or milk to form a firm dough. Turn out on to a lightly floured surface and form into a round scone shape about ¾-inch thick. Brush with beaten egg and place on a lightly greased baking sheet. Bake for 15 to 20 minutes until golden. Serve with butter. Traditionally this barley bread was cooked on a griddle or in a frying pan in a similar way to Singin' Hinnies.

Norham Castle

Overnight Spice Cake

When baking days had to be carefully planned, mixtures were often prepared overnight, to give the raising agent time to work and to ensure that oven temperatures were correct. This is a County Durham recipe.

1 lb plain flour	2 teaspoons mixed spice
2 oz butter	2½ teaspoons bicarbonate of soda
6 oz lard	
8 oz caster sugar	8 oz currants or sultanas
4 oz ground almonds	8 oz raisins
½ pint sour milk	

Grease and line a 9-inch cake tin. Sift the flour into a bowl and rub in the fats until the mixture resembles fine breadcrumbs. Stir in the sugar, ground almonds, spice, bicarbonate of soda and fruit, combining well. Add the milk and mix to a soft dough. Place in the prepared tin, cover lightly with a clean tea-towel and leave to stand overnight. The next morning, set oven to 325°F or Mark 3 and bake the cake for 1 hour. Reduce the oven temperature to 300°F or Mark 2 and bake for a further 1 to 1½ hours, covering the top with a piece of kitchen foil if it appears to be browning too quickly. Allow to cool in the tin for 10 to 15 minutes, then turn out on to a wire rack.

Stanhope Fruit and Nut Cake

A rich fruit cake containing black treacle, traditional to County Durham.

8 oz butter, softened	4 oz chopped walnuts
8 oz caster sugar	4 oz chopped dates
3 eggs	5 oz raisins
1 lb plain flour	5 oz sultanas
¾ teaspoon baking powder	5 fl oz milk
	1 oz black treacle

Set oven to 350°F or Mark 4. Cream the butter and sugar together in a bowl until light and fluffy, then beat in the eggs, one at a time. Sift the flour and baking powder together and fold in, then add the nuts and fruit, alternately with the milk. Warm the treacle slightly and stir in, combining the mixture well. Spoon into a greased and lined 9 to 10-inch cake tin, smooth the top and bake for 2 hours, covering the top with a piece of kitchen foil if it appears to be browning too quickly. Allow to cool in the tin for 10 minutes, then turn out on to a wire rack.

Panjotheram

This curiously-named casserole, made with mutton chops is native to County Durham and was traditionally served at sheep-killing time.

8 lamb chops, trimmed
1½ to 2 lb potatoes, peeled and sliced
3 onions, peeled and sliced
1 pint beef stock, slightly thickened with a little flour
Salt and black pepper

Set oven to 325°F or Mark 3. Dust the chops lightly with a little seasoned flour. In a deep casserole, arrange layers of the potatoes and the onions, seasoning each layer. Bring the stock to the boil and pour over sufficient to come halfway up the vegetables. Arrange the chops on top of the vegetables, cover with a lid and cook for 1½ to 2 hours, adding more hot stock as necessary. Serve with carrots and a green vegetable. Serves 4.

Barnard Castle

Felton Spice Loaf

A traditional Northumberland high-tea loaf.

4 oz butter	**4 oz self-raising flour**
4 oz sugar	**½ teaspoon mixed spice**
2 eggs	**2 oz candied peel, finely**
2 oz ground almonds	**chopped**
4 oz plain flour	**6 oz sultanas**

A little milk

Set oven to 375°F or Mark 5. Cream the butter and sugar together in a bowl until light and fluffy, then beat in the eggs one at a time. Fold in the ground almonds. Sift together the flours and mixed spice and fold into the mixture. Stir in the peel and sultanas and add sufficient milk to give a soft, dropping consistency. Turn the mixture into a well-buttered roasting tin and smooth the surface. Bake for 30 to 40 minutes. Cool for 5 minutes in the tin, then turn out on to a wire rack. Serve sliced, plain or very lightly buttered.

Durham Cutlets

A recipe for using up left-over cooked beef, shaped into cutlets and fried in breadcrumbs. Traditionally, Durham Cutlets were decorated with paper cutlet frills.

1 lb cooked beef
1 onion, peeled and finely chopped
½ oz butter
3 oz fresh white breadcrumbs
Grated rind of half a lemon
1 dessertspoon chopped fresh parsley
Pinch of nutmeg
Salt and black pepper
1 teaspoon brown sauce
1 egg, lightly beaten
Egg and breadcrumbs for coating
Oil for frying
Macaroni pieces
Chopped fresh parsley for garnish

Mince the beef. Fry the onion in the butter until soft, then mix with the beef in a bowl. Stir in the breadcrumbs, lemon rind, parsley, nutmeg, seasoning and brown sauce and combine well. Add sufficient beaten egg to bind, then, on a lightly floured surface, form the mixture into traditional 'cutlet' shapes. Brush with beaten egg and coat with breadcrumbs. Heat the oil and fry the 'cutlets' until golden brown. Drain on kitchen paper and keep warm. Just before serving, insert a piece of macaroni into the end of each cutlet to represent the 'bone' and serve garnished with chopped parsley and accompanied by creamed potatoes and a green vegetable. Serves 4.

Leek Pudding

A suet pudding filled with chopped leeks, served as an accompaniment to stews in Northumberland.

**1½ lb leeks, weighed when cleaned and trimmed
1 lb prepared suet pastry   2-3 oz butter
Salt and black pepper**

Chop or slice the leeks finely. Lightly grease a 1½ to 2-pint pudding basin and line with the pastry, reserving a portion for the lid. Place the leeks into the basin, dot with the butter and season. Cover with the reserved pastry, sealing the edges well and tie down with lightly buttered greaseproof paper and kitchen foil. Place in a saucepan of boiling water and steam for 1½ to 2 hours, topping up the water as necessary. Turn the pudding out of the basin and serve in slices as an accompaniment to a stew or casserole. Serves 4.

High Force, Teesdale

Bacon Floddies

*Served with sausages and eggs as a breakfast or supper dish,
Floddies are traditional to Gateshead.*

8 oz peeled potatoes	2 oz self-raising flour
2 medium onions, peeled	Salt and black pepper
6 oz streaky bacon, de-rinded and finely chopped	2 eggs, beaten
	4 tablespoons oil *or* 1½ oz bacon fat

Grate the potatoes, squeeze out any liquid and place in a bowl. Grate the onions, or chop very finely and add to the potatoes with the chopped bacon, flour and seasoning. Mix very well together. Stir in the eggs. Heat the oil or bacon fat in a large frying pan. Put tablespoons of the mixture into the pan and fry steadily for 5 to 8 minutes, turning once, until golden brown and cooked through. Drain on kitchen paper and keep hot until ready to serve with the fried sausages and eggs.

Oven Bottom Cake

A roughly shaped cake from County Durham, originally made with any left-over dough after a baking session.

**1½ lb plain flour   ½ teaspoon salt   ½ oz fresh yeast   ½ tablespoon sugar
¾ pint warm water   4 oz lard   A little warm milk**

Sift the flour and salt together into a bowl. Combine the yeast with the sugar and a little of the water until creamy. Make a well in the flour and add the yeast mixture with the remainder of the water. Combine well, then turn out on to a lightly floured surface and knead for 5 to 10 minutes until smooth. Form into a ball, place in a bowl and cover with a clean tea-towel. Put in a warm place to rise for 1 hour or until doubled in bulk. Turn out on to a lightly floured surface and knock back. Knead lightly, then cut a quarter piece off the dough. Cut the lard into cubes and push into this cut-off piece of dough. Replace the lard-filled dough into the main piece and knead it in roughly, using the knuckles of one hand, forming the dough into an irregular shape that it will retain during baking. Place on a greased baking sheet, cover with a clean tea-towel and leave to prove for 30 minutes. Set oven to 425°F or Mark 7. Bake for 10 minutes, then reduce the oven temperature to 375°F or Mark 5 and bake for a further 30 minutes until golden brown. Brush with warm milk to glaze. Serve hot, cut into irregular pieces, with butter and jam.

North Country Tart

An open tart layered with raspberry jam and an egg, coconut and golden syrup mixture.

8 oz prepared shortcrust pastry
2 tablespoons raspberry jam
2 oz butter   1 oz caster sugar   1 oz golden syrup
4 oz desiccated coconut   1 small egg, beaten

Set oven to 375°F or Mark 5. Roll out the pastry on a lightly floured surface and use to line an 8-inch pie plate, trimming the edge neatly. Spread on the raspberry jam. Melt the butter, sugar and golden syrup together in a saucepan over a low heat, then stir in the coconut and beaten egg. Combine well together and spread on top of the jam. Bake for 25 to 30 minutes or until the filling is set and the pastry golden. Serve hot or cold. Serves 4 to 6.

Dunstanburgh Castle

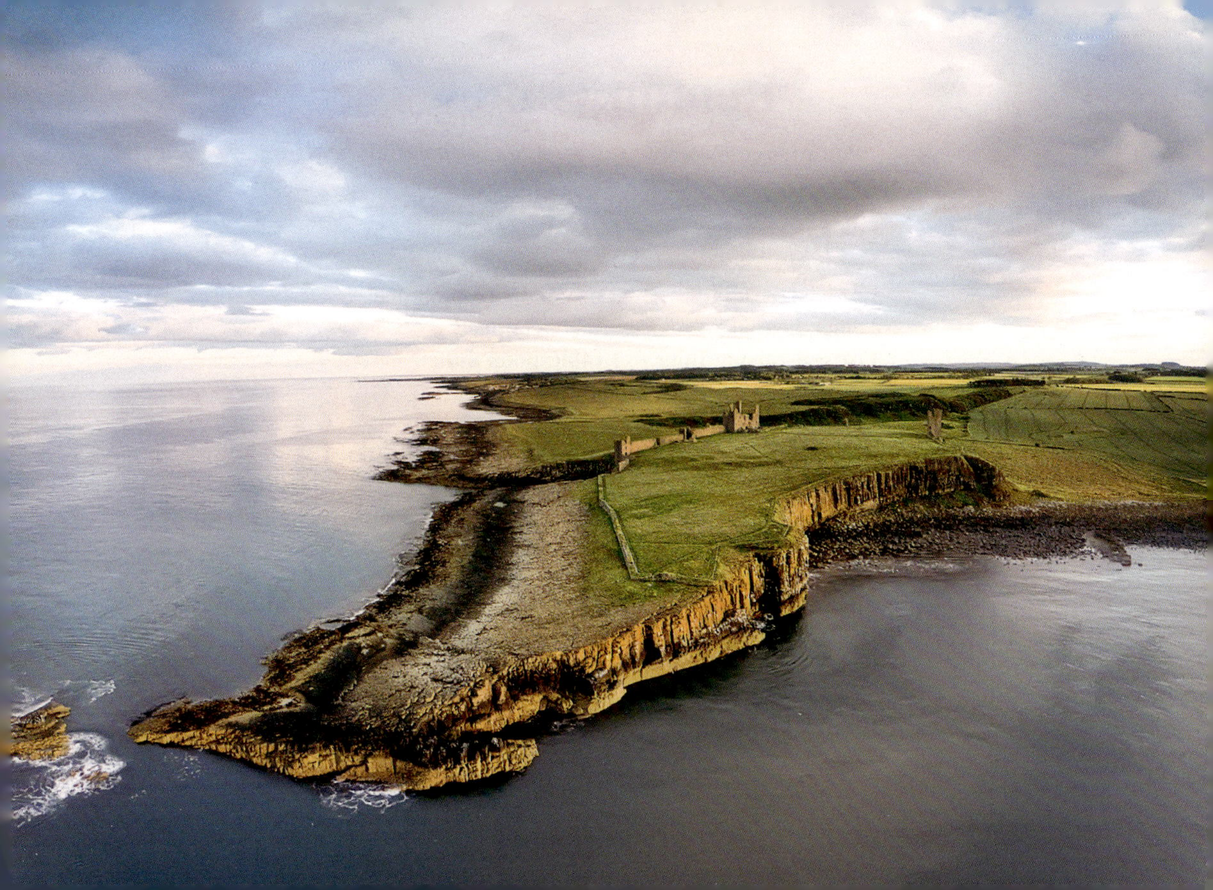

Lemon Cake

A rich lemon cake topped with sugar. A similar cake is found in neighbouring Cumberland.

4 oz butter, softened
2 oz lard
5 oz caster sugar
2 eggs, beaten
8 oz self-raising flour
Grated rind and juice of a lemon
2 oz candied lemon peel, finely chopped
1 tablespoon milk
A little sifted icing sugar

Set oven to 350°F or Mark 4. Grease and line a 7-inch cake tin. Cream the butter, lard and sugar together in a bowl until light and fluffy. Add the eggs, a little at a time with a little flour and mix thoroughly. Fold in the rest of the flour. Add the lemon rind and juice, the candied peel and milk and mix thoroughly; the mixture should be of a dropping, yet firm, consistency. Put into the tin and smooth the top. Bake for 1 to 1½ hours, until a thin skewer inserted into the cake comes out clean. If the top appears to be browning too quickly, cover with a piece of kitchen foil. Cool in the tin for 5 minutes, then turn out on to a wire rack. Serve dredged with a little icing sugar.

Celery Cheese

A Northumberland supper dish.

**1 large head of celery, wiped and trimmed
A little milk   Salt and black pepper
3 to 4 oz grated Cheddar cheese
1 large egg, beaten   1 oz fresh white breadcrumbs
A 'walnut' of butter**

Grate or chop the celery very finely and place in a saucepan. Pour over sufficient milk to cover and season. Simmer gently for 10 to 15 minutes or until the celery is tender, then leave to cool. Stir in the cheese and beaten egg and turn into a well-buttered ovenproof dish. Set oven to 350°F or Mark 4. Sprinkle the breadcrumbs over the celery mixture and dot with butter. Bake for 10 to 20 minutes until golden brown. Serves 4.

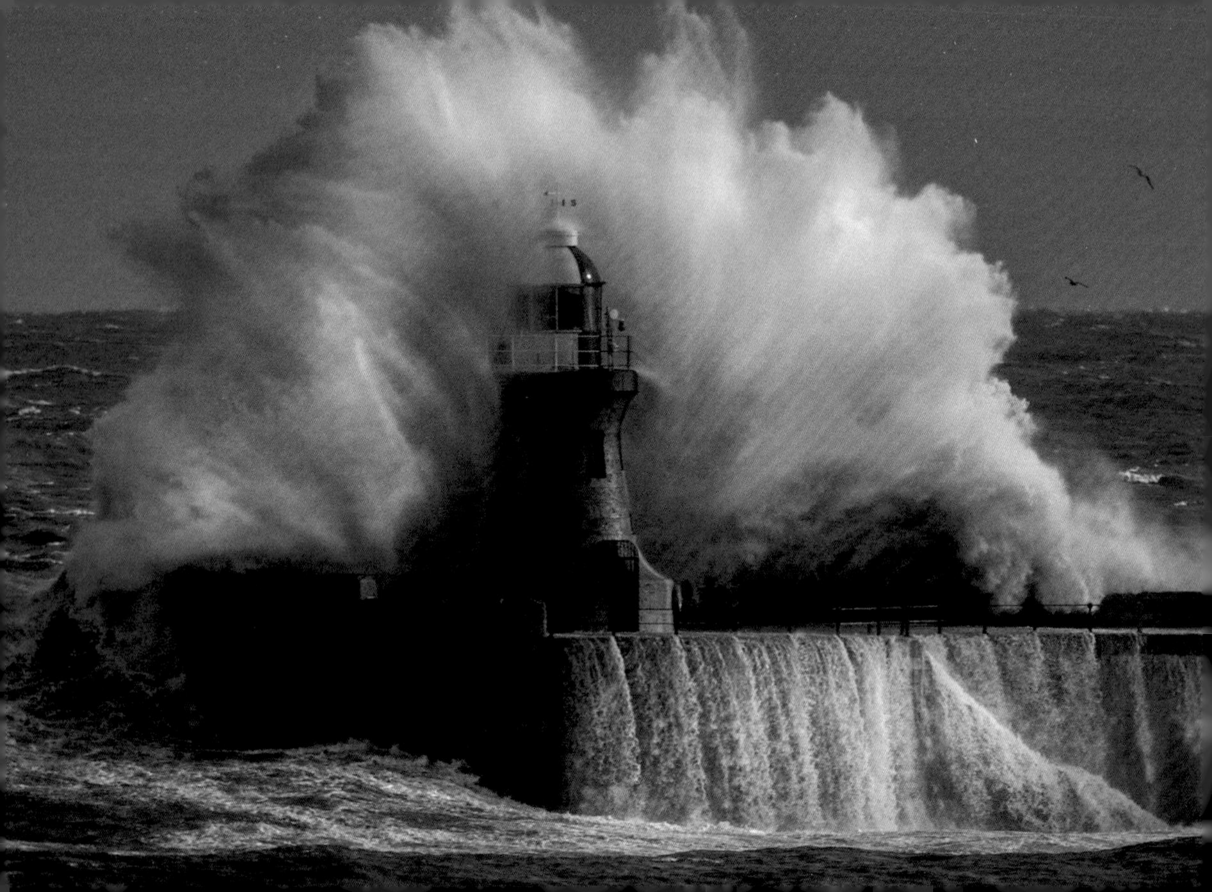

Alnwick Stew

*A Northumberland stew made from chopped bacon forehock
layered with onions and potatoes.*

**2 lb bacon, forehock or end collar
3 onions, peeled and chopped
1-1½ lb potatoes, peeled and sliced
English mustard powder   Black pepper   A bayleaf
Chopped fresh parsley for garnish**

Cut the bacon into cubes, about 1 to 2 inches. Place a layer of onions in the base of a large, heavy-bottomed saucepan, add a layer of bacon and then add a layer of sliced potatoes, seasoning each layer with a little mustard powder and pepper. Continue layering and seasoning and finish with a layer of potatoes. Place the bayleaf on top and pour in sufficient cold water to come just below the top layer of potatoes. Cover with a lid, bring to the boil, then simmer very gently for 1 to 1½ hours. Serve the stew garnished with chopped parsley and accompanied by boiled carrots. Serves 4 to 6.

South Shields

Whitley Goose

A traditional dish from Whitley Bay which has nothing to do with real geese!

4 onions, peeled and left whole
4 oz grated Cheddar cheese
Black pepper   ¾ pint single cream
A 'walnut' of butter

Place the onions in a saucepan and cover with lightly salted water. Bring to the boil and boil for 15 to 20 minutes or until the onions are tender. Drain well and allow to cool a little. Set oven to 400°F or Mark 6. Chop the onions roughly and mix with half the cheese. Season. Butter an ovenproof dish with the 'walnut' of butter and pour in the cream. Lightly stir in the onion mixture and top with the remaining cheese. Bake for 20 to 30 minutes, or until golden. Serve as an accompaniment to cold meat or ham. Serves 4.

Alternatively, this will serve 2 as a supper dish, accompanied by crusty bread.

Tasty Batter Pudding

A popular Northumberland farmhouse pudding.

1 oz shredded suet	2 tablespoons sugar
4 oz plain flour	½ teaspoon mixed spice
Pinch of salt	1½ oz sultanas or currants
2 eggs, beaten	1 pint milk

Set oven to 350°F or Mark 4. Mix the suet, flour and salt together in a bowl. Make a well in the centre and stir in the beaten eggs. Add the sugar, spice and fruit, then stir in the milk until the batter is combined well. Pour into a well-buttered 2-pint pie dish and bake for 1 to 1¼ hours, covering the top with a piece of kitchen foil if it appears to be browning too quickly. Serve in slices, accompanied, if desired, by stewed fruit. Serves 4.

This pudding can be converted into a savoury dish by omitting the sugar, spice and fruit and serving it as an accompaniment to roast meats, especially pork.

METRIC CONVERSIONS

The weights, measures and oven temperatures used in the preceding recipes can be easily converted to their metric equivalents. The conversions listed below are only approximate, having been rounded up or down as may be appropriate.

Weights

Avoirdupois	Metric
1 oz.	just under 30 grams
4 oz. (¼ lb.)	app. 115 grams
8 oz. (½ lb.)	app. 230 grams
1 lb.	454 grams

Liquid Measures

Imperial	Metric
1 tablespoon (liquid only)	20 millilitres
1 fl. oz.	app. 30 millilitres
1 gill (¼ pt.)	app. 145 millilitres
½ pt.	app. 285 millilitres
1 pt.	app. 570 millilitres
1 qt.	app. 1.140 litres

Oven Temperatures

	°Fahrenheit	Gas Mark	°Celsius
Slow	300	2	150
	325	3	170
Moderate	350	4	180
	375	5	190
	400	6	200
Hot	425	7	220
	450	8	230
	475	9	240

Flour as specified in these recipes refers to plain flour unless otherwise described.